Made in United States
North Haven, CT
11 December 2021

12385647R00065